P9-ARF-449

ALTERNATIVE ENERGY

SOLAR ENERGY

GRAHAM RICKARD

Gareth Stevens Children's Books
MILWAUKEE

Titles in the Alternative Energy series:

Bioenergy
Geothermal Energy
Solar Energy
Water Energy
Wind Energy

For a free color catalog describing Gareth Stevens' list of high-quality children's books, call 1-800-341-3569 (USA) or 1-800-461-9120 (Canada).

Library of Congress Cataloging-in-Publication Data

Rickard, Graham.
    Solar energy / Graham Rickard.
        p. cm. — (Alternative energy)
    "First published in the United Kingdom, copyright 1990, by Wayland
(Publishers) Limited"—T.p. verso.
    Includes index.
    Summary: Explains how the Sun, which is the ultimate source of all
energy on earth, can be used to provide electricity and power.
    ISBN 0-8368-0709-X
    1. Solar energy—Juvenile literature. [1. Solar energy.] I. Title. II. Series:
Alternative energy (Milwaukee, Wis.)
    TJ810.3.R53   1991
    621.47—dc20   91-9261

North American edition first published in 1991 by

Gareth Stevens Children's Books
1555 North RiverCenter Drive, Suite 201
Milwaukee, Wisconsin 53212, USA

U.S. edition copyright © 1991 by Gareth Stevens, Inc. First published in the United Kingdom, copyright © 1990,
by Wayland (Publishers) Limited.

Picture acknowledgements

Artwork by Nick Hawken

The publishers would like to thank the following for supplying photographs: David Bowden, 10; Chapel Studios,
4; Mary Evans, 11; Eye Ubiquitous, 16, 20; Jimmy Holmes, 19; National Power, 26; Neste Advanced Power
Systems, 22; Oxfam, 21 (lower); Science Photo Library, 12, 13; Topham, 21 (upper); U.S. Department of Energy,
25 (both); Wayland, 6, 23; Zefa, cover, 4, 5, 7, 9, 14, 19.

Editors (UK): Paul Mason and William Wharfe
Editor (U.S.): Eileen Foran
Designer: Charles Harford
Consultants: International Solar Energy Society and Gabrielle Wollfit

Printed in Italy

1 2 3 4 5 6 7 8 9 95 94 93 92 91

Contents

Words that appear in the glossary are printed in **boldface** type the first time they appear in the text.

WHY ALTERNATIVE ENERGY?

Energy is the ability to do work. All animals and plants need energy to live. All machines need energy to work. As the world's population increases and people use more machines, more energy is needed to power them. The demand for energy has increased more than ten times since the beginning of this century.

Most of this energy is produced by burning one of three **fossil** **fuels** — oil, natural gas, and coal. But there is only so much fossil fuel in the world. Supplies that took millions of years to build up are being used at the rate of over half a million tons an hour. At this rate, all the world's oil and gas will be gone by the year 2040.

Fossil fuels also cause serious damage to the environment. When they burn, fossil fuels produce poisonous gases that

These Indonesian oil workers are pumping oil that cannot be replaced.

Sunbathers in the Canary Islands enjoy the heat of the Sun.

An open coal mine in Australia. Coal mines like this one are very ugly and are often criticized by environmental campaigners.

turn into **acid rain**. Acid rain pollutes vast areas of the world, killing trees, fish, and wildlife. Some of these gases also contribute to the **greenhouse effect**, which is gradually warming up the Earth's **atmosphere**.

Because of all these problems, people all over the world are looking for alternative sources of energy. Some people see the use of **nuclear energy** as the best alternative to fossil fuels. But nuclear energy depends on supplies of uranium, which is even rarer than the fossil fuels we use now. Also, the pollution caused by nuclear energy is far more dangerous than anything produced by fossil fuels.

So scientists and environmentalists are working together to come up with safe, clean, and renewable sources of energy.

There are many natural sources of energy all around us. The power of the Sun, wind, and moving water of tides and rivers all provide clean, renewable energy, if we can only come up with ways to use it. This book looks at the different ways of using solar energy. As long as the Sun's rays reach the Earth, the energy of the Sun cannot be used up. If we can find good ways of using the energy the Sun gives us, we will have a power supply that is safe, cheap, and clean, and that will last for billions of years.

THE POWER OF THE SUN

About 93 million miles (150 million km) from our planet, there is an enormous power source emitting vast amounts of energy into space. It is the Sun, the source of all energy on our planet. Trees, for example, use the Sun's energy through **photosynthesis**. When they die, their wood can be burned to release this energy as heat.

Humans get their energy from food crops, which need sunlight to grow.

The Sun has a powerful influence over our climates and weather systems. For example, the Sun's rays **evaporate** water from the sea. This evaporation forms clouds, which drop their moisture as rain. Rain replenishes the

Vast amounts of energy being released as heat and light by a forest fire. This energy originally came from the Sun.

land and continents and restores essential nutrients. Without the Sun to initiate the process of evaporation, the Earth would be arid and uninhabitable. Also, without the Sun to keep the oceans warm, they would freeze solid, and the land would be so cold that life could not exist.

The Sun has a powerful influence on the weather, causing winds and rain.

However, if the amount of energy that the Earth gets from the Sun increased, there would also be problems. The ice at the North and South poles would melt and the seas would rise, and large

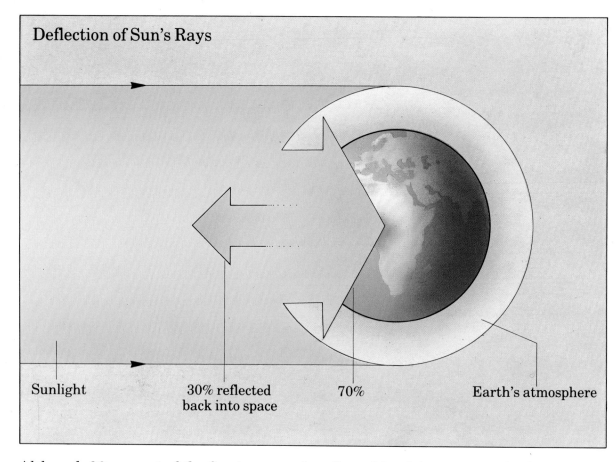

Deflection of Sun's Rays

Sunlight   30% reflected   70%   Earth's atmosphere
back into space

Although 30 percent of the Sun's energy is reflected back into space, the Sun showers the Earth with more energy in an hour than is used as fuel in a year.

areas of land would be drowned. This is why people are worried about the greenhouse effect.

The Sun is more than a million times larger than the Earth, and is about 864,000 miles (1.4 million km) wide. The Sun is so far away that its light takes eight minutes to reach the Earth. If you imagine the Sun as being the size of a basketball, the Earth would be the size of a tiny pebble.

The Sun is mostly made of two gases: hydrogen and helium. The hydrogen becomes helium in an enormous atomic reaction that releases vast amounts of energy. Every second, 564 million tons of hydrogen become 560 million tons of helium. The remaining four million tons are released as energy. This release of energy happens at the center, or core, of the Sun, where the temperature is 29 million °F (16 million °C).

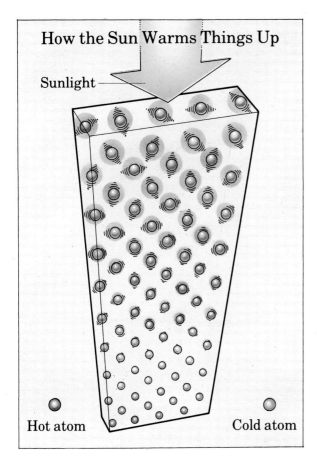

How the Sun Warms Things Up

Sunlight

Hot atom

Cold atom

The Sun heats objects by making their atoms move fast.

When the Sun's rays reach our atmosphere, about 30 percent of their energy is reflected back into space. The remaining 70 percent reaches the Earth's surface as heat and light. The Sun releases more energy onto the Earth in one hour than all the world's people consume as fuel in a year.

Although the Sun's rays are not actually hot, they do warm objects by stirring up in them the tiny particles, called **atoms**, that all things are made of. When stirred up, the atoms move faster and produce heat. Light-colored objects absorb less heat than do dark objects, because the light objects reflect the Sun away from themselves, while dark objects absorb the Sun's rays. So if you touch a black car on a sunny day, it feels hotter than a white car.

A solar flare leaps thousands of miles into space. The Sun constantly releases huge amounts of energy.

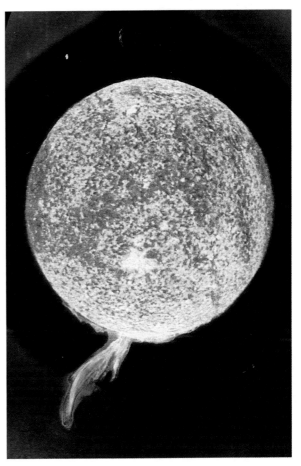

HARNESSING THE SUN'S POWER

People have been using the Sun's energy for thousands of years. The first people lived in caves facing the Sun. The Sun warmed the caves in cold winter months. They also used sunshine to dry animal skins and cloth. Over 3,000 years ago, a king's palace in Turkey was warmed by using water heated by the Sun. Around A.D. 100, the Romans harnessed the Sun's heating power in their homes by laying dark, thick floors. These floors absorbed and stored the Sun's heat, which came in through the windows during the day. The floors released the stored heat at night.

This solar water heater warms water to a temperature of 190°F (88°C).

For centuries, the Sun has been used to dry things like this Bangkok silk.

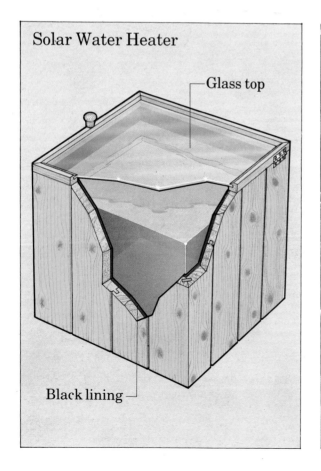

Solar Water Heater

Glass top

Black lining

This picture was printed in 1882. It shows a solar-powered printing press, which was used to print a newspaper, named the Sun, *in France.*

Early farmers preserved their crops and meat by drying them in the Sun. Farmers all over the world still do this today. African, Mediterranean, and Asian peoples still use the Sun's heat to evaporate seawater, which produces salt.

The first solar **furnace** was built in France in 1714. Soon afterward, the Swiss scientist Horace Benedict de Saussure built the world's first solar water heater. This solar water heater was simply a wooden box with a glass top and a black base. By absorbing the Sun's heat, the water in the box reached a temperature of 190°F (88°C). In 1774, the French scientist Antoine Lavoisier focused sunlight through a series of high-powered lenses to produce heat. In 1878, also in France, a dish-shaped mirror was used to focus solar heat onto a boiler, which in turn produced steam to drive a printing press. Around the same time in Chile, a machine powered by the Sun produced fresh water by evaporating seawater.

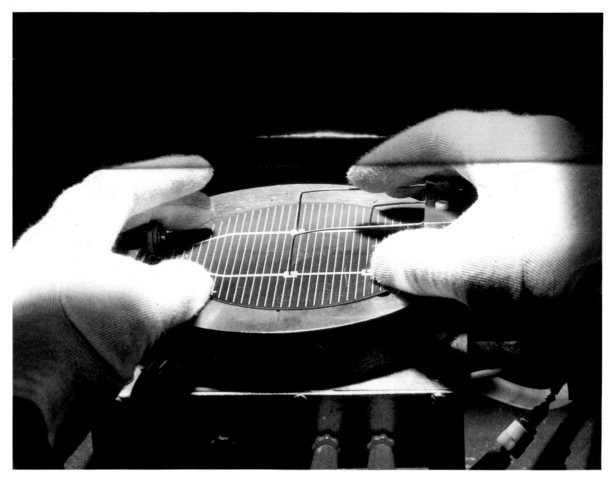

A solar cell being made in Caen, France. The multicolored sheet in the middle is the cell, which is crossed by thin wires that pick up the electricity generated by it.

The first **solar cells**, which change sunlight into electricity, were developed in the 1880s. These solar batteries were not improved until the 1950s, when two U.S. scientists produced solar cells that worked well — but were also very expensive.

The National Aeronautics and Space Administration (NASA) saw solar cells as the most efficient way to provide electricity in space. In 1959, *Vanguard 1*, the first satellite to use solar power, was launched.

In the 1970s, an energy crisis led to an increase in researching ways to use sunlight to make electricity. Through this re-search, the cost of solar cells was reduced by 90 percent. Solar cells were also made to work better.

This man, who lives in a mountainous area of China, is lining up his solar cells so that he can watch television.

Today, they are used in many household items, such as watches and calculators, and are used to generate power in isolated places.

Every year, the Sun gives us ten times more energy than is stored in all the world's reserves of coal and oil. When fossil fuels, such as coal, natural gas, and oil, are depleted, solar power will play a large part in replacing them.

There are many problems to overcome, though, before the Sun can be considered as an efficient alternative energy source. Sunshine, although plentiful, is very difficult to collect in a usable form. Today, a large city would need solar collectors that take up as much land as the city itself to get a sufficient amount of power. Also, sunlight is weak or non-existent at the times when we

Solar collectors like this one take up a lot of land and are eyesores to people who prefer the fields that they were built upon.

need energy most — at night and in the winter. So we must find ways of storing solar energy.

The Sun's energy is free. Devices for collecting the Sun's energy use no fuel, cause no pollution, and are easy to maintain. They do present some **environmental** problems, however. Solar power stations take up large areas of land. They are not very attractive. The materials needed to build these power stations, such as metal, glass, and plastic, all need a lot of energy for their own production. **Silicon**, which is extracted from sand or quartz and is used in solar cells, is obtained by mining sand. Mining sand can destroy whole areas of land and can upset the delicate balance of the environment.

Electricity generated by solar power is very expensive, but will become cheaper as fossil fuels become more expensive or run out. Solar energy now accounts for only 1 percent of worldwide electricity production, but this figure may rise to 30 percent

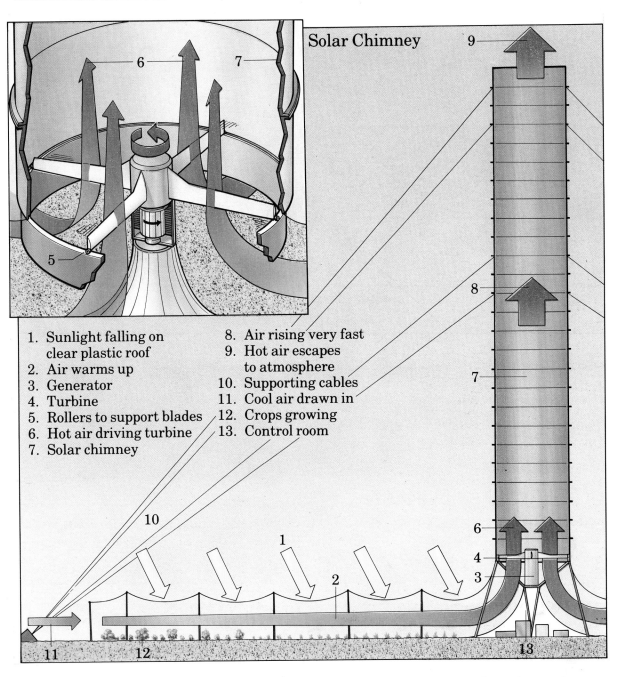

Solar Chimney

1. Sunlight falling on clear plastic roof
2. Air warms up
3. Generator
4. Turbine
5. Rollers to support blades
6. Hot air driving turbine
7. Solar chimney
8. Air rising very fast
9. Hot air escapes to atmosphere
10. Supporting cables
11. Cool air drawn in
12. Crops growing
13. Control room

by the middle of the twenty-first century.

Solar chimneys using **turbines** are another way to use the Sun's power. Solar chimneys use the Sun's rays to heat the air under a transparent roof. Today's solar chimneys are not very efficient, and until they can be made to work better, they will be used for experimental purposes only.

SOLAR HEAT COLLECTORS

A solar wall. The dark area behind the glass is heated by the Sun. The glass keeps the heat inside the house.

In cold climates, houses are usually built facing the Sun, which supplies over one-fifth of all heating needs. In the Northern Hemisphere, this means that the windows face the south.

This heat can be prevented from escaping by **insulating** the walls and roof, and by using windows with two layers of glass. A glass-covered area, such as a **greenhouse**, can trap even more of the Sun's heat.

A new French design can provide warm air as it is needed. In a house, a wall facing the Sun is painted black. This black wall absorbs a lot of heat. An outer layer of glass stops heat from escaping. The Sun heats up the wall and produces a rising column of warm air, which circulates through the house. Because the wall holds the heat for several hours, the system continues working after dark and during cloudy periods, when it is most needed. People who live in similar houses in England have found that their heating bills went down by 50 percent when this system was in use.

Some solar heating systems use collectors to get heat from the Sun, and a liquid, such as water or oil, to take away the heat and store it for later use. The best-known type of collector is the flat

Although solar panels like this one cannot heat water to a very high temperature, they can supply most of the heating needs of homes in sunny climates.

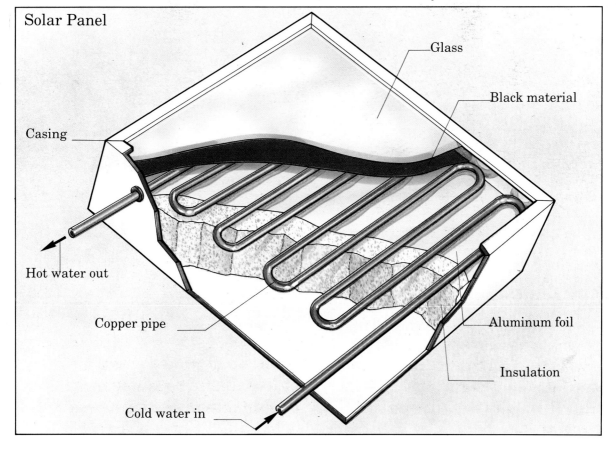

Solar Panel

Glass

Black material

Casing

Hot water out

Copper pipe

Aluminum foil

Insulation

Cold water in

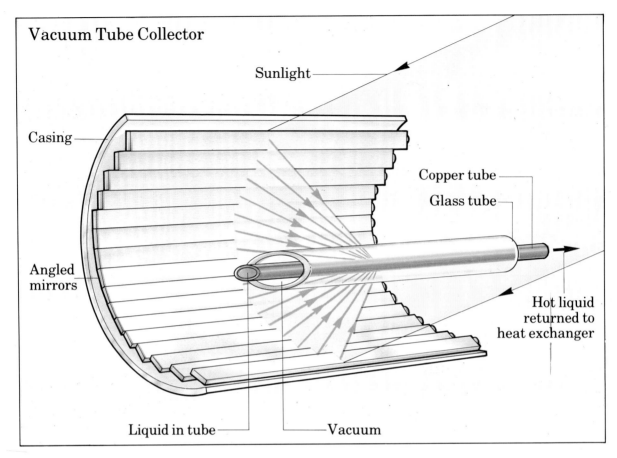

Vacuum Tube Collector

Sunlight

Casing

Copper tube

Glass tube

Angled
mirrors

Hot liquid
returned to
heat exchanger

Liquid in tube

Vacuum

Vacuum tube collectors heat liquid to high temperatures.

plate collector, or solar panel, which is often mounted on a roof. The solar panel acts like a radiator in reverse, absorbing rather than emitting heat. The panel is made of a black metal absorber plate with a series of tubes attached to it. These tubes are inside a flat, insulated box with a glass cover. The Sun's **radiation** passes through the glass and heats the absorber plate. Water in the tubes heats up and is piped to a storage tank, which is wrapped in insulating material. Cool water flows in through another pipe and is heated in the collector. These collectors cannot reach very high temperatures, but in warm climates they supply most of a household's hot water needs and reduce fuel costs.

A **vacuum** tube collector works better than a solar panel, producing temperatures of up to 572°F (300°C). A heat-absorbing fluid passes through a tube inside a metal heat collector. The collector is inside a sealed glass container, through which no air can enter or escape.

Collectors that concentrate the Sun's energy by focusing its rays onto a small area reach the highest temperatures. Some have curved reflectors which focus the rays onto tubes containing water to absorb the heat, and some use flat mirrors. Small, curved dish reflectors are now used as solar ovens by campers and by families in countries where there is often a shortage of firewood.

Central receiving stations use hundreds, or even thousands, of flat mirrors to collect the Sun's rays. The mirrors direct the rays to the top of a central tower. A liquid, such as pressurized water, oil, or molten metal, flows through the tower and carries the heat to make steam. The steam drives turbines, which run electric generators. These large receiver stations, also called "power towers," can produce very high temperatures. They are already being used to produce electricity in Europe, Japan, and the U.S. (see pages 24-25).

A solar panel in Tibet. Solar panels can replace firewood as a heating source.

These roofs in Israel are covered with solar panels.

19

ELECTRICITY FROM SUNLIGHT

Light from the Sun, as well as heat, can be used as an energy source. Solar cells change light directly into electricity. Most solar cells are made of silicon. Solar cells have two separate layers, each with an electrical charge. When light hits the cell, these electrical charges begin to move between the two layers. This produces a very small amount of electricity.

Because each cell produces little electricity, it takes many cells to produce enough electricity for most uses. On a sunny day, panels of cells can produce about 100 **watts** of electricity per square yard (0.84 sq m).

Solar cells are already being used to power isolated lighthouses and navigation beacons. They have also been tried out on different kinds of vehicles.

Because they are up in the Himalayas and power lines cannot reach them, many Tibetan villages like this one rely on solar energy.

Panels of cells like this are portable and can easily be used wherever there is sunlight.

In 1981, a light plastic plane flew from Paris to England in five hours, powered by 16,000 solar cells on the wings and tail. In 1986, a solar car, called Sunrider, was driven from Athens, Greece, to Lisbon, Portugal, traveling at about 19 mph (30 kph) and powered by 300 solar cells.

Panels of solar cells need little maintenance and are useful for providing power in remote places that do not have a constant supply of electricity. Some parts of the world, such as California, Spain, India, and Saudi Arabia, have many hours of sunshine. In these sunny places, houses and even entire villages depend on solar cells for electricity.

Solar cells are used to pump water from this well in Africa.

In Africa and Asia, where doctors travel from village to village, solar panels are used to power the portable refrigerators that store their medicine. In California, several large solar power stations have rows of solar **arrays** that move to track the Sun across the sky. Two of these stations each generate enough electricity to supply a small town of 3,500 homes.

Because the Sun's rays are much stronger outside Earth's atmosphere, solar cells are much more effective in space than on Earth. Solar cells have long been used in the space industry to power satellites and space stations.

This camel is carrying a refrigerator full of medicine across the Sahara Desert. The refrigerator is powered by solar cells.

Large-scale solar power stations like this one in California are becoming more common. They can generate large amounts of power.

Someday, it may be possible to build an enormous solar power station in orbit around the Earth. The solar station would carry millions of solar cells and would be constructed in space from parts delivered by spacecraft. The Sun's light would be turned into powerful beams of energy, called **microwaves**, and sent back to Earth. Once the microwaves reached Earth, huge receiver stations would convert them into electricity. Building such a power station would be very expensive and difficult, but the station could produce huge amounts of electricity.

SOLAR ENERGY IN ACTION

The Solar One power station

California, the world leader in replacing fossil fuels with alternative energy, has canceled all plans to build nuclear and coal-fired power stations. Instead, it is trying to develop the use of solar energy and wind energy. Using solar energy to make steam to power turbines began near Barstow, California, in the late 1970s and led to the building of Solar One, the world's largest and most expensive solar power station. Solar One began producing electricity in 1982.

Solar One is a central receiving station, or "power tower." More than eighteen hundred mirrors

Turbines are used in almost all large-scale solar power projects.

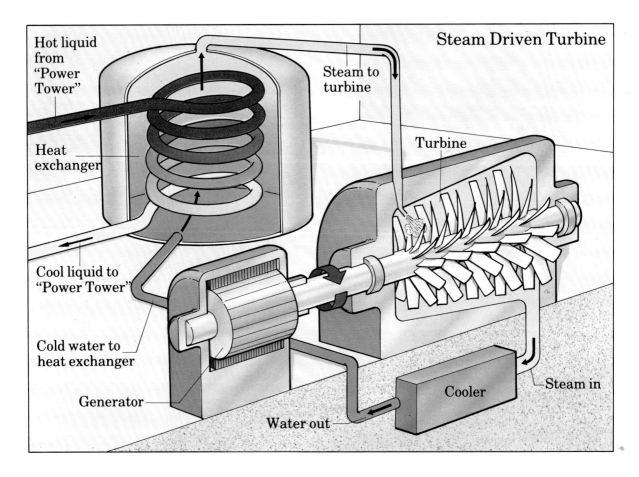

Hot liquid from "Power Tower"

Heat exchanger

Cool liquid to "Power Tower"

Cold water to heat exchanger

Generator

Water out

Steam to turbine

Steam Driven Turbine

Turbine

Cooler

Steam in

Rays of light reflected away from the boiler at Solar One.

are placed in semicircles around a 256-foot- (78-m-) high tower. The mirrors focus sunlight onto the boiler, which is located at the top of the tower. As the Sun moves through the sky, the mirrors turn around, following it. Oil in the central collecting tower heats up and is piped to a power plant. There, it heats water to 572°F (300°C), producing steam. The pressure of the steam turns a turbine, which powers a **generator** to produce 10 **kilowatts** of electricity.

Solar One was very expensive to build. By around 2010, however, the electricity produced by such solar stations could cost the same as we now spend converting fossil fuels to energy. As fossil fuels

The boiler at the top of the tower is white-hot.

diminish, they will become difficult to obtain, and solar power will be cheaper by comparison.

The solar furnace at Odeilo, France. The mirrors on the hillside concentrate the Sun's rays onto the large mirror. This focuses them farther, onto the furnace at the top of the tower.

The Odeilo solar furnace

Although power towers can reach high temperatures, solar furnaces are able to get even hotter. They collect energy over a wide area and focus it on a single spot.

Solar furnaces are ideal for scientific experiments, which can be affected by the impurity of the fuel used to heat them. The Sun's energy is pure.

The best-known solar furnace is at Odeilo, France. Curved mirrors cover one side of a ten-story building, forming one large mirror, which focuses the Sun's rays onto an area of less than one square yard (0.84 sq m). Eleven thousand flat mirrors on the opposite hillside move to follow the Sun, reflecting the Sun's rays onto the large, curved mirror. A tower in front of the building is the target area and is the focus of all the rays, where temperatures can reach 5,970°F (3,300°C).

Storing the Sun's energy

The Sun does not shine — or is weakest — when heat is most needed, at night and in the winter. Therefore, solar energy must be stored. There are several ways to store the Sun's energy.

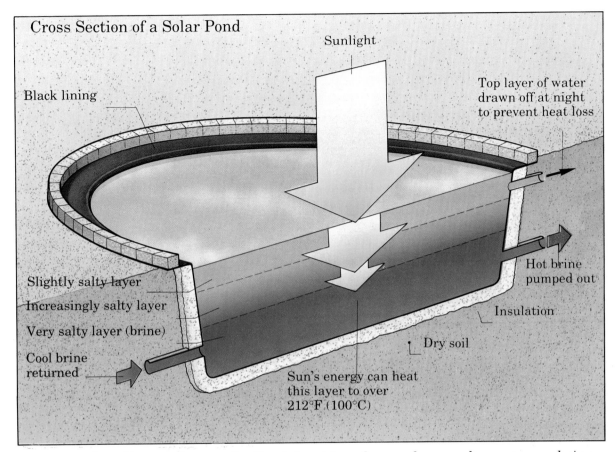

Cross Section of a Solar Pond

Sunlight

Black lining

Top layer of water drawn off at night to prevent heat loss

Hot brine pumped out

Insulation

Slightly salty layer

Increasingly salty layer

Very salty layer (brine)

Dry soil

Cool brine returned

Sun's energy can heat this layer to over 212°F (100°C)

Solar ponds collect and store the Sun's heat in a layer of very salty water, or brine, at their bottom.

A solar pond is both a collection and storage system. It has a dark, heat-absorbing layer at its bottom and is filled with layers of brine (salty water).

The Sun's heat is absorbed by the black lining and passes to the bottom layer of brine. The heat is trapped by the upper, less salty layers of brine. The hot brine can be pumped to wherever the heat is needed and then returned to be reheated.

Solar ponds store heat long after the Sun has set. Therefore, they are very useful for heating at night. Solar ponds are cheap to build and to use, and can be quite large.

Unlike fossil fuel supplies, the Sun cannot "run out" as a source of energy. But it's up to us to keep on devising ways of harnessing its incredible power and putting it to use for ourselves here on Earth.

PROJECT

You will need:

- A strong cardboard box

- A piece of thick cardboard

- Aluminum foil

- Tape

- A straightened wire coat hanger

- Two nuts and two bolts

- A hot dog

- Cork

- Heavy stones

How to make your own solar cooker:

1. To make the frame of your solar cooker, cut out the top and one side of a strong cardboard box as shown.

2. Using very thick cardboard, cut a circle the same height as your box, and then cut the circle in half. Cut a strip of cardboard, slightly shorter than the length of

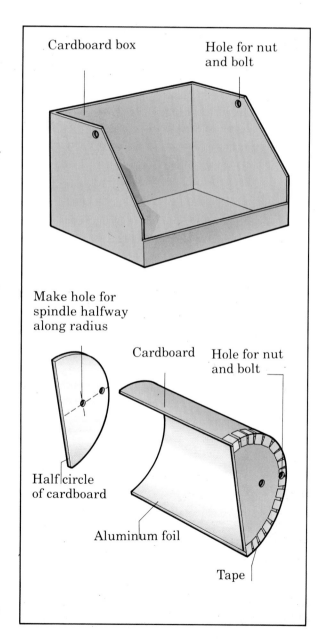

Cardboard box

Hole for nut and bolt

Make hole for spindle halfway along radius

Cardboard

Hole for nut and bolt

Half circle of cardboard

Aluminum foil

Tape

Cork

Nut and bolt

Stones

the box, and wide enough to fit around the curved edges of the half circles.

3. Tape the aluminum foil to one side of each half circle and the strip of cardboard.

4. Tape each end of the cardboard to one of the half circles, with the foil facing inward. You have now made a half tube. Attach this to the frame with the nuts and bolts, as shown in the diagram.

5. Pass a spindle of thick wire through each end of the half tube.

Put the stones in the bottom of the box to make it more stable.

6. Remove the wire spindle halfway, push it through the hot dog, and reattach it. Point the foil lining of the half tube toward the Sun. Turn the spindle so that the hot dog cooks evenly.

Warning:

The hot dog is not the only thing that will heat up! Be careful when you touch any part of the cooker, especially the stones, the wire, and the nuts and bolts.

Glossary

Acid rain: Rain formed when pollution in the air combines with water vapor in clouds. It kills trees and wildlife, and, in time, will even eat away stone.

Array: A large group of mirrors or solar cells.

Atmosphere: The layer of gases that surrounds a planet, moon, or star.

Atoms: The tiny particles that combine to make up all the elements.

Environment: The things that make up a place.

Evaporate: To turn a liquid into a gas.

Fossil fuels: Energy sources, such as coal, oil, and natural gas, formed from the remains of plants and animals that lived millions of years ago.

Furnace: A device for heating something, such as a home, or for melting things like glass, metal, or pottery.

Generator: A machine that generates, or produces, electricity.

Greenhouse: A glass-covered room attached to a house, which can be used for solar heating and growing plants.

Greenhouse effect: The warming of the Earth through the production of gases that trap the Sun's heat.

Insulate: To prevent heat from escaping.

Kilowatt: A thousand watts of electricity.

Microwaves: Radiation made up of very tiny, short waves.

Photosynthesis: The process by which plants use sunlight to help make their own food.

Radiation: Energy in the form of rays. Light, x-rays, and microwaves are all types of radiation.

Silicon: The element that is found in sand and is used to make solar cells. Silicon is the second most common element in the Earth's crust. Oxygen is the most common.

Solar cell: A tiny silicon battery that changes sunlight into electricity.

Turbine: A device, shaped somewhat like a propeller, which turns to power an electric generator.

Vacuum: A space that contains no air.

Watt: A unit of electrical power. It takes 60 to 100 watts to power most light bulbs.

Books to Read

Catch a Sunbeam: A Book of Solar Study and Experiments.
Florence Adams (Harcourt Brace Jovanovich)
Done in the Sun: Solar Projects for Children. Ann
Hillerman (Sunstone)
Energy from the Sun. Melvin Berger (Harper & Row Junior Books)
Hot Water and Warm Homes from Sunlight. Alan Gould (Lawrence
Hall of Science)
How Did We Find Out about Solar Power? Isaac Asimov (Avon)
Power from the Sun. Lawrence Abrams (Dillon)
Solar Energy. Sheila Kaplan (Raintree)
Sun Power: The Story of Solar Energy. Madeleine Yates (Abingdon)

Places to Write

These groups can help you find out more about solar energy and
alternative energy in general. When you write, be sure to ask specific
questions, and always include your full name, address, and age.

In the United States:

**Conservation and Renewable
Energy Inquiry and
Referral Service**
P.O. Box 8900
Silver Spring, MD   20907

Renew America
1400 16th Street NW
Suite 710
Washington, DC   20036

In Canada:

**Efficiency and Alternative
Energy Technology Board
Department of Energy, Mines,
and Resources**
580 Booth Street, 7th Floor
Ottawa, Ontario   K1A 0E4

**Solar Energy Society
of Canada**
#3, 15 York Street
Ottawa, Ontario   K1N 5S7

Index

A **boldface** number means that the entry is illustrated on that page.